part one

for information on the author and more written + visual
stimulation find, follow + tag euni online at

www.notwithoutdirt.com
@euniquedeeann

books may be purchased for business or promotional use.
for more information on bulk purchases or commissioned work,
please contact eunique deeann directly via the web link above.

a collection of personal journals, letters, and poems to those that i have come to love over time.

in no particular order, each piece stands on its own. may it bring you inspiration, healing, and a connection to your own understanding of the layers of love.

this book is dedicated to
my mother, my father.
my step mom and step dad.

to the ones that grew them,
the ones that they grew to love.

to my past lovers and the ones who
taught them how to love.

to mother nature who without hesitation has
always been unconditionally welcoming.

and lastly, to myself.
who from the beginning of our time
and until forever,
i am on a journey with to
open up, let go, and let in.

all, for the sake of connection, understanding,
and a commitment to love.

———————

———

everyday i fall in love.
sometimes a million times over,
sometimes with you.

———

---

look into my eyes
stare until the answers come.
kiss my lips
gently
firmly
press until our insides spark.

hold my hand
grip it firm and strong.
send me serenity.
answers, confirm.

never leave my side
unless it is to come closer,
to go deeper inside.

———

sometimes all you can see is the clouds,
even though the sun is shining bright behind them.
look a little deeper my love,
you'll be surprised how much one ray
can warm your heart.

———

———

desires so intense my brain shuts off,
my heartbeats collide.

———

———

i told you once that i have seen the lowest of my
lows and i would never go back. what i lacked was
my highest of highs. there, i went with you without
turning back.

———

---

curiosity lead me to you,
desire to know something new.
for a discovery of somewhere unknown.

your simplicity and skill kept me intrigued from
the first meeting of our eyes. entrapping my gaze,
touching my soul. conversation natural, opening,
true. i found myself too quickly drawn to you.

it was easy, i felt as if i knew you.
that i wanted to. and this, you wanted also.

as you locked your eyes on mine, you jumped into
my soul. touching me deeply - beneath the surface.
keeping a deep hold on the unspoken.

feeding my desire to ease into a new unknown.
despite the closeness i felt with you, i felt
apprehensive, postponing things i wanted to be
true. the feeding of my desire to ease into a new
unknown. uncertain of the things i could have
wanted with you.

attraction strong, chemistry unspoken.
yet still guarded. by secrets of the world external,
pre-existing to our meeting.

and as close as we were in the moments we created.
distance blocked our connection further than any
instant explanation.

still, a new love and lover you were to me. a new
infatuation to entice me. my mind confused by the
heart's self-fulfilling prophecies. your blue eyes
beamed, peering deeply into my everything.

the only regret i have is not being your first love,
and you not being the one to fulfilled my need to be
idolized by the one who shares my bed.

———

how long can i grieve you before
i'm no longer allowed to feel?

———

i found myself in you.
i am afraid i will lose my nerve
to get closer to her without you.

———

i see you avoided my eyes -
because this is where our truth,
our soul, our bind lies.

and in order to separate
you had to be the first to untie.
to release me
and let me begin to fall
to realize that i don't need your hand
or you by my side.
to take off, to expand, to fly.

———

———

your eyes,
your lashes,
your lips,
tranquility surrounds me.
as i catch you smile
slightly from the corner of your mouth
i cannot contain my touch.

goodbyes are like hellos,
an ending to something discovered.
an introduction to something new.

as it is all the same,
when i stare out into the water,
this is where i leave my heart.
this is where i am close to you.

———

let me know i am the one who keeps your feet on the
ground.

———

twelve

————

i want someone to love the ugliest parts of me
the same as they do the sunshine that pours out
endlessly.

———

pain is temporary.
but the ability to truly feel,
to love,
is longer than the lifespan of a soul
engulfed in the body
that hosts it
for a short span of days.

i saw her.
you loving her.
her loving you.
and it was beautiful.
it was painful.
and my heart closed.

i know you want my story to be the same as yours.
my blood to bleed thick + red like wine.
my heart to ache as deeply as you felt once before.
my eyes to cry rivers that flow south and line the
trails you've left behind.

i know you want my agony to be one that we can
dwell in like yours.
my rage to pour out from every opening.

but no. this is not it.
excuse me while i find my voice.
while i unravel my own to tell.

———

it's quite mind blowing how you've come so quickly
into my life and taken over such large real estate.
entangling your human, your body, mind + soul with
mine. you were not quite what i was expecting, but
even more so surprisingly, such an exact version of
what i truly need.

everyday, i am thankful that you picked me. and
everyday i find happiness in knowing that i have
this chance, at this moment, in this place in my life
to share, grow, learn, love + expand with you.

by no means do i expect this to be easy. but i know
in time, as we continue to peel back each other's
layers, we will exist more fluidly, with greater ease.

you are challenging me to be a better person, and
i hope you can say the same. i want nothing more
right now than to be the best versions of me, to be
able to share that with you in the minutes we have.
the spaces we reside. and the memories we make.

as i've gotten to see some of the sides of you, i've
grown to understand some, at the surface, of what
challenges you.

i know it's scary. that it's hard.

to think what it could possibly feel like to re-live
things that so strongly impacted us in our pasts.
to open up, let in, let go. forgive. reshape memories,
feelings, emotions. all the things that have defined
us and made us who we are. what we are. what we
know. to be challenged to change.

the challenge to expand and redefine everything we
know, have known, seems scariest, maybe because
there's a feeling of if we let go of the past, it will not
exist - which means neither will we.

———

―――――

but what if the purpose of expanding, letting go,
letting in is so that we can experience everything
fully. so we can be present. become bigger, fuller,
freer. what if the purpose of our pasts, our pains, is
simply, most simplistically, so that we can learn how
to feel most deeply.

so that in that moment that the best thing you could
ever imagine comes to surface, you see it. you stop
to really take it in. you feel it, deeply. the same,
even more greatly, than the pain that has held you
down.

you see, love and pain are one in the same.

they have the power to shape us, shift us, break us,
define us and make us into another version of the
human we came here to be.

at some point, we realize that this is the most
powerful thing we will experience in any lifetime
and we let go and give into love - or pain - and this
molds how we spend all of our days. chasing, giving,
receiving and anticipating either extreme.

in the days leading up to me letting you in, i chose
love. and in this decision, i started healing my
perceptions of pain. with full testimony, i tell you,
this more often than i'd like to admit is an
intentionally, forced effort. but everyday, this is
my biggest effort. everyday, i try.

and through all the attempts, i've learned i have to
love me before i can share or expect this from
anyone else. on my worst days, i've often
disconnected from all the things i have said in these
pages. and on my best, is when i rediscover myself.
it's when i let the things out of my head, out of my
heart without any needs, demands, intentions or
expectations.

―――――

i have done this most by putting pen to paper. filling notebooks cover to cover. i've discovered more about me and the world here than i have any other ways.

we seem to have built a relationship shaped on the trust of being apart. admittedly, this still shakes me. but i thought, maybe instead of giving into my pain and fear, what if i could try to open up, let out + let in. and when i can't find the words to express to you in voice or in person, maybe i could write to you and leave you with all the bits of me that i often feel so guarded to reveal.

and when i leave, i will leave you with these words. and if you get nervous, you can read the pages + feel me close. remembering the roots of how i truly feel. and as words in the moments are so challenging at times, perhaps you can do the same for me. we can stay connected, no matter if we are together or far apart.

because the more we let out - the good + the bad - the more space we have to receive, ask for, and accept what we want and need. when you are ready, know that this is a safe space for you to sink into.

and know that i have coated this space with more love than i could have ever imagined i could share with or give to someone. i'm happy that this someone is you.

tomorrow, i will return home to you. to be present. with you. in this moment. forever. for always. for now.

———

love is free.

———

i feel at peace when i am with you.
old souls, reunited.
no longer split in two.

———

———

heart filled to the brim
or drained empty
it all
hurts, feels, bleeds
just the same.
deeply.
and in vain.

i walk.
one foot in front of another
snowy mountain roads.
dusty desert paths.
in search for something deeper
than each step i passed.

contemplating,
what if.
i cut myself open.
to expose all that lies inside.
what if.
i bled out all that haunts me.
to see what else is left to hide.

———

what you put out towards me,
into me,
you will receive.
i am just an external reflection of
everything your heart longs for.
of all the things your soul aches for and needs.

———

twenty one

———

i am strong enough to handle your honesty,
no matter how brutal it may be.
but i am not weak enough to accept your lies.

look me in the eyes, expose your truths
and trust that my response will be the same.

if you are strong enough to love me,
then love me as i am
and reveal your weakest,
most vulnerable places to me.

in this you will see
the best of you
the best of me
binds in honesty
and the depth of intimacy
that soars beyond what others will be able to
comprehend.

———

twenty two

———

what do you see when you look at me,
green eyes filled with mystery.
hands tough with craftsmanship
heart of gold.
my mind spins in search of things i could
have surely missed.

silent stares
peering into my soul.
heartbeats deepen as trust unfolds.
sharing moments and making memories with time.
listening to my everything as if it is not just mine.

———

twenty three

as i look back into your eyes,
i can feel something once unfamiliar.
something becoming known,
something growing to stay.

when i am away from you i still see your eyes.
piercing through me.
it's not hard to recognize where you are
when we are apart.

when you are away,
i feel the same as if you were here.
never unsure,
never insane
steady, secure.

these are the things i unveil.
when i close my eyes,
i see your eyes
still staring back into mine.

———

no one tells you
that letting go
hurts the same as
letting in.
both come with
understanding
heartaches
by sinking + giving in.

————

i send you my love
and pray that you too are working
to open your hardened heart.

so that even if i'll never know,
you'll find a time to fall apart.

———

the distance between us had nothing to do with how
i feel about you. i love you unconditionally. the
distance we feel has to do with me loving me and
you loving you. we cannot control that for each
other. that is why we walk alone. if you want, when
you want, when you're ready. walk towards me,
reach out grab my hand.

·

rebuilding the empire created too many days ago to
count is becoming easier with each breath exhaled.

forgetting the betrayals,
replacing the distress.
sorting,
surrendering
to the beauty that brings
unrest.

boldly and bravely,
with no other choice,
i move forward.

bit by bit,
i do not take what was remaining.
rather, i scatter it along the path
as i move on.
creating a trail from what was,
to lead the way towards what will become.

i walk a path overgrown by nature,
no longer safe for return.

so forward and onward i go now,
only with vague memories of
what has happened.
i lay new footsteps to outline
what is to come.

———

listen, love.
the agony of letting go is only a temporary distress.

lean in.

———
twenty nine

———

you were not meant to be long term.

———

———

if you feel -
search.
seek.
find.
all that you are looking for.

if you feel -
do not stop.
until you find all that you are missing.

and when you are ready.
come back home,
settle into the space
i am growing,
openly for you.

———

———

don't lose your own sight of you.
dont lose your own connection
to your roots.
you are pure.
you are true.
you are beautifully, magically.
wonderfully
growing you.

———

thirty two

———

we're all fucked,
you're nothing special in your chaos.
but i'll tell you this
i'm not wearing my scars as makeup
disguising myself as a clown.

stitch by stitch,
i am unraveling my wounds
rewriting the story that someone else thought
my life would be.
creating what my life will become.

you can take me tattered,
or you can toss me with all the others
that your presence has worn.
either way.
i am what i am, unconditionally.
a little rugged,
a little torn.

———

thirty three

———

listen carefully.
you can not need me.
you will not survive.

———

———

my heart aches
longing for anything other than ordinary.

———

it's true.

i want more than most things to be with someone.
to share my space, my heart.
my fears and fantasies.
my longing, love, the depths of my soul.

but this someone,
they must really understand,
must really, truly see me.
for who i am.
for what i am here to do.
and what my existence means.

if you are that someone,
you will know without any doubts,
that the aching my heart holds,
has nothing to do with you.
the longing my soul seeks,
has nothing to do with you.
that the searching my eyes take
and the pondering my mind makes.
this, has nothing to do with you.

if you are that someone,
you will know that being welcomed into my space
means that everything that i need outside of me,
outside of my longing to shift the world,
i find in you.

———

thirty six

―――――

don't fret.
just because our love doesn't look like theirs
or feel how it did once before
doesn't mean it's not real.
doesn't mean it won't last.

―――――

———

i will never get over you, blue eyes.
even though we spent so many months
in the black.

all i will ever remember is
those two nights
the three days
that we forgot the world existed
outside of us.

that time we came together.
shared our secrets,
opened up and into each other,
relaxed, released, became free.

oh, what i would give to have
one more hour there with you
where nothing else mattered
but you and me.

———

i included you in my sexual rotation out of drunken
desperation. for lust, for must, for calming the
feeling that i would bust, i let you devour me.

my body tingled from the influence of shots of
tequila and cheap beer. leaving my to mind to
wonder, mirroring your fingers discoveries of the
unspoken mysteries found within me.
separate, in part, but still equally true.

disconnected to connect, together, somatically as
one. the physicality of the sexuality we created was
prolific only in this moment in time. but in reality,
it was nothing more than a stimulation for
penetration. a meditation i used often to numb the
pounding of my head, my heart. our bodies matched
the rhythm, just to pass the time.

i drown my sorrows in the liquids of denial.
strangle my repressions in the entanglement of our
limbs. my stems wrapped tightly around your waist.

your hands brush against my face. over and over,
it does not matter the place as long as you take me
away from this state of agony, actuality. even if only
temporarily. cloud my mind, help me unwind.

right or wrong, i don't have a care. as the only
purpose for you also is to escape with me through
the loss of control. in reality. my current state is
no place to be. in reality. your current state had no
concern for me. and consciously, i return this lack
of care, ruthlessly.

abused, misused. we share this addiction to
affliction. a state of carnal connection was the
greatest state we could accomplish.
torn, disconnected. sensuality, confused for love.

this, tied us together. but once the buzz wore off,
and the sun rose to shine a new day on you and i,
nothing changed. even though we still lie together,
side by side. we were still separate, and in the light
of day, strangers, even more so, in every way.

———

thirty nine

———

circling, challenging
needing to know.

breathing through
the pressures,
of the thought
to let you go.

———

———

jump the gun
explosions of words.
sentiments resurface.
grasping for answers.
feelings of regret.

here i stand, alone.
holding deep onto
the belief that you are meant to be.
sinking deeply into
the thought that you do care for me.

———

like the waves build up, gaining strength as they
approach the shore. my heart pounds heavy, full of
love, passion and lust. longing for the same
release brought to the mighty ocean when the
current breaks. flooding rocks on the shoreline,
singing a rhythm of peace.
my longing for you is never ending,
my love continues on.

but like the sea wall, full of power and persistence,
my heart too is evolving.

and like the waterfront, without the support of the
wind or exchange of the revolving earth.
the strength of this love shifts, never leaving you
in solitude, but redirecting its force to pound a new
coastline with the same consistency i once gave to
you.

———

forty two

the longing does not fade with time.
i want to be with you.
feel your heartbeat in my chest.
your breath rise my ribcage.
feel you from the inside.

the one who shatters your desolitions,
and turns it all into a smile.
the one who you want to be with.
at this moment in time.
let me be the one.

you say one of the best things about me is my smile.
it's faded now, missing from view.
it left my lips and has been tarnished
along with the pieces of my heart
you took out the door with you.

———

as the sun tucks away behind the clouds
and the night steals the day. the sadness that
replaced the space you used to live in my heart
races to catch up with me, covering the grounds i
passed just hours before.

it takes over the minutes of darkness leaving me to
pray for daylight to return sooner so i can hit the
road and put distance between us once again.

hoping that this time,
in this daylight
i will be able to get away.
in these hours to greet the next night to come
with the same eagerness
as i greet the morning's sun.

———

although there is such a tough shell,
there's a delicate one guarding being
hurt, abused, played for a fool.
and if it is to feel fully
or to limit life's experiences,
you, my love, you would rather be numb.

———

i can't protect you from your fears
i can't become small and hide.
but i can show you a new way
to open up
and release the insecurities
that you hold inside.

———

in your presence
or in your arms
when i feel your touch
hear your breath.
no matter what
i have no regrets.

———

i tell myself that sometimes you meet people at the
wrong time. that sometimes you will meet again in
the future. sometimes you need time apart to grow.
to understand that you must let go.
in order to spread your own wings.
to understand what it is to be free.

and sometimes.
maybe this sometime,
the one your heart longs for will come back
to find you and take you too.

but in those time that it is not this sometimes,
i tell myself that i will survive.
that i must know in this i will be finding the truth
that is best for me.
and you are doing this for you.

i tell myself to remember.
to believe that nothing is ever lost.
only shifting, becoming refined.
as we are now living life separately.
i hope you are telling yourself this too.

———

———

opening the heart doesn't mean
that you will receive love.
it means you are releasing fear.
vulnerability.
insecurity.

———

there are days that i need you.
your love, your advice, your strength.
that is what family is.

but i know that with or without you,
my foundation will not be as it was once defined.

that i will stand on my own two feet.
rooted and strong.
and i will continue on my path,
growing, evolving, bringing into my life
every chance i can
everything i need.

to replace the rocks that have been compromised
where you once stood.

i just want
to be me.
and in this.
not be held
responsible
for someone
else's happiness
or agony.

i just want
to be me.
is this too
much to ask?

―――――

i am still connected to you.
heart broken by you.
unsure of why or what to do
with
or without you.

―――――

———

i don't trust you with my heart or my
vulnerability. and if i can't be vulnerable with you,
i can't be myself. if i can't be myself, i don't know
who i will be. but we've seen the other versions. and
those are not true to me. these alter egos are
putting distance between us. keeping me closed off,
us living separately.

———

if we can find the way to let go
of the past.
forget about the future.
and be here,
in this moment.
be here,
now.
all that matters.
will matter.
if we're here,
in this moment,
all that matters is right now.

―――――

you are my foundation.
regardless of the proximity of this connection.
i am here to heal your soul.
and i will shift my thoughts in connections to you.
to only send you love, healing, softness, support.

you are teaching me to love,
to trust in this.
to confidently follow my heart without necessity
for an answer in the immediate.
order and process.
to put myself top of mind.

that relationships worth having
are grown over time.
by patiently allowing the other to process.
to accept,
to open up their space,
to welcome you in.

―――――

———

we talk of finding soulmates, the other half of our
heart. but you see, the heart is designed with veins
because the heart isn't divided into halves. rather,
it is made of thousands of pieces. this is why it
breaks. this is why it aches. this is why it beats,
stretches and then, this is how it grows.

i began learning this the day i met you. that the love
one holds in their heart isn't dedicated to just one
person or only one thing. it isn't based on
geography or attached to any specific feeling.
that unconditional love flows, through and through.

this is why i call you little roots. because from the
day we met, you not only helped ground me, but
through this, you have been helping me discover
how to open up and expand my heart.

she shouted,
screamed,
enraged with pain.
i stared, silently.
breathed deeply.

leaned slightly forward to say;
"i see you. i hear you. i understand."

"what?" she twisted,
confused with anger.

"you are appreciated.
you have done well.
i know this.
we all do.
and we honor your path.
the sacrifices you've made every minute to
ensure ours would be smoother than the one you
just passed.
thank you."

i am coming home to you.
my heart is heavy.
but not with jealousy, insecurity, rage.
it is filled with sadness knowing that your heart
too is heavy, healing.
knowing that your heart has been
re-broken.
old wounds
reopened.

my heart is so heavy as i am so far away.
understanding that you may need me.
my stillness.
my touch.

stay steady, my love.
i am coming to you.
i am sorry i didn't see the details at first.
through my own selfish eyes. that i didn't realize
how deeply you might need to go in order to heal.

but nonetheless,
i will have your back.
be by your side.
hold the space for you
to take the time.
with this.
with everything.

———

love is not our own.

to be able to open up and give the love you hold
to another is selfless.
it is strong.
not everyone holds this strength or understands.
so be kind.
be gentle.
and if you are strong,
be vulnerable.
open your heart,
share the love you store inside you
with those who seek it.

because love is not our own.
love belongs the broken souls.
it is for giving them hope
to help them return home.

———

open up your eyes
look into mine.
breathe me in
show me all you hide inside.

———

———

numb.
numb without feelings.
your touch is distant.
i am cold.

without feeling.
isolated.
my touch is surface,
you have somehow become unknown.

isolated.
isolation.
only alone.
surface conversations
blindly fill the time.
words empty.
like the meeting of our bodies
and exchange of our touch.

you stare right at me
and me,
right through you.

———

sixty three

———

my love for you runs deeper than the shallow
breaths i gasp for each moment, every single day.

my love for you is unbound. unexplainable to the
common. my love for you is greater than my need
for air.

———

go deep,
deeper.
this is where the pleasures
smothers the pain.

———

each moment that passes.
every time our nervous eyes meet.
my heart putters caution.
warning that you are not ready,
to fully reveal yourself with me.

a hesitation lingers,
desire grows for more time to
dig deeper inside.
looking for a confirmation
that this time,
i will wait for you.

for the moment
when you are ready,
to open your space.
with authority,
and lead me nearer to you.

understanding that
in the time it takes,
you will patiently wait for me.
that if i grow weary,
and need you to stay steady.
you will return this act
and give me the space i need.
believing when it's right,
i'll let you know,
by welcoming you
to take the lead.

———

you want your freedom to be in chaos and bounce from one thing to the next. i'll let you go. let you free. because opening up for you is damaging me.

———

———

i felt everything with you. you brought me to life,
gave me the things i never had before. the issues
came when you started to believe that you were
not enough for me. that you couldn't give me what i
wanted or needed. and the truth is all i ever wanted
or needed was you. i found everything outside of me
in you, with you. and without you, i have not been
the same.

―――――

we did not separate in our own growth
to a better place.

we grew apart, into the place of darkness.

but this distance never disconnected us.
as you have become a part of me.

and although i stray away,
i could never take the light to leave you
alone in darkness,
without knowing that you've found
another way out of the black.

open up your eyes, love.
find your way back.

―――――

i send you my love
and pray that you are also working
to soften your hardened heart.

so that even if i'll never know,
you'll find time to fall apart.

and through this open up.
to see the child you have hidden
deep inside.

that you'll give her permission
to come out
to grow up,
a reason to no longer hide.

that in turn,
and over time,
you'll let go of all that distanced
you from you,
you from her,
you from me.

———

even in the depth of darkness, you will find love.

———
seventy one

———

i've seen your heart,
i know your soul.

there is no such thing as purity
my love. breathe easier.
your being, like all others, is colored.

with character, stories, struggles, and varied
interpretations of connection.
i want you to know that i have nothing but that type
of love for you.

and this love begins and ends each day,
with the rising and setting of the sun.
it carries over into the days that have yet to come.

and with each moment,
i aim to overflow you, to drown you in affection.
for you to be reborn in nothing but love.

leaving behind murky waters
made by all that has tainted you,
that has made you feel anything
less than whole.

———

———

i want to discover you.
bring you comfort and ease.
provide a space that you can feel and find peace
being just as you are.

to feel safe and secure here
in opening up, in being you.

to stop living this life scattered,
straddled,
confused.

to find your roots,
confidence, consistency
in the space
that i am holding right here for you.

———

green eyes,
stare deep into mine.
let your hands caress me
our minds,
intertwine.
your lips, let them meet mine.
and our bodies dance to music
deep within our souls.
your instincts, let them be ravenous.
settle your cravings deep within mine.
our intimacy, unfold.
firmly, own your sensations.
slowly,
silently,
read my mind.
open me up,
our hearts, let them bind.

———

seventy four

i went out.
searched.
explored.
opened up.
closed off.

i cried.
broke down.
became dead inside.

i was afraid.
unsure.
unstable.
insecure.

and in this moment, i found you.
who stood, steady by my side.
and here next to you i realized.

all i was looking for
was someone who would try to love me
as much as i would try to love them.

———

there are many souls aching.
feel dear ones.
there are many hearts breaking.
understand, you are not the only ones.

your existence isn't for you to hold selfishly
but to give fully,
experience deeply,
love limitlessly.
go ahead,
feel my loves.

———

you stranger.
i owe you nothing.
but i'm here.
open and rawly giving.
my heart
in every footstep.
hoping
you follow behind.

———

———

we are the same, have always been.
i see you, lost and lonely.
i can tell you from my own discovery,
what you're seeking you will never find.

because it's not hiding outside.
it's buried deep within you.
beneath the turmoil
you've caked up over time.

can you look yourself in the face,
in the eyes?
and with honesty say,
i have nothing to hide?

going back,
means opening up.
letting it all out.
sitting still to sink,
deeply within.

and when you do, take the time.
tear it all down. rip it all up.
and pour it all out.
every. single. inch.
pull it apart.

until your raw, broken, aching.
that's the love you've been seeking.
that's when the healing begins.
this is where you'll find the space
to see everything outside of you.

this is where the loneliness,
the pain ceases to be.
where you'll find comfort
in the living, letting go, letting it be.

———

———

do you know what it feels like to love someone
who does not love you back?
to feel isolated, trapped by this misuse of
exchanging affections.

emotionally, romantically, entangled by your own
accord. drowning in your own lust. need for love.
a solo affection for one who does not know that
you too exist.

do you know?

———

i see you.
and understand.
that you may not feel yourself,
or be behaving as you normally would.
but you are still here.

and i see that you are
beautiful, pure.
at the core.

misaligned, disconnected
you might feel at present.
but you,
without hesitation are more connected
truer, to you
than ever before.

---

blue-eyed mystery, you whisper to my soul from far
away. painting, transforming timeless snapshots of
your genius into beauty. colorful glimpses of
something grander than the life i am living.

i silently beg of you. leave me like a portrait,
paralyzed by the visions that your fingers trace. i
am desperate for them to touch me like they have
touched nothing else. to paint my skin like a mural.
top to bottom. redefining each imperfection.
lighting the darkest of the corners. just like the
canvas you have investment in that you effortlessly
overtake. this, i long for too.

blue eyed mystery, as i watch you, curiously
waiting. to see what you create. your brush strokes
whisper to my soul much closer than i can take.

———

life.
it's showing on you.
in you.
in your skin.
every wrinkle.
your furrowed brow.
guarded heart.
perception, wirey.
like your nimble, worn fingers.
crippled at every extension,
from each deception you've handed out.

———

my heart aches for you often.
and when i speak of you
it's typically with tear filled eyes.

but if your curiosity gets the best of you
and you find yourself in search of me
know that i am happy.
i am full.
grounded.
wholly unveiling myself.

know that i am no longer drowning in the sorrows
from forced connection
bound by a lifetime of manipulation and selfish lies.

———

i want to know what it feels like to be close,
to be intimate
without opening my legs.
what it feels like to let my heart be touched
without the caress of my thighs.
to allow someone to go deep
without penetrating me.
to expand our minds beyond
intertwining our limbs and hidden sides.
there has to be a greater love.
a purer love.
than just letting you come inside.

———

―――――

not everything is about love.
some things are logic.
and these things, i do not understand.

―――――

i hope you find a way to prioritize yourself. not the
tasks that keep you busy. or your consumptions that
help you shove everything down. not with activities
that deflect and distract. but truly, find priority for
you. your health. your healing. your purpose, path,
and reasoning for being here in this moment in
time. in this place, on this earth. to walk, one step
in front of the next, down the trail that waits for
you. i hope as you run away, that you go heal. with
each step that you take, you pick up the pieces
scattered over time, and in this uncover all the
missing parts of you.

———

we all deserve a chance to receive love
bigger than we're able to give.
a chance to give love
more than we are able to receive.
let down our walls.
to let it out.
to let it in.

―――――

i get it
i see
how you didn't want to open yourself up to be seen.

so you ran
and hid
put distance between you and me.

because you knew
i was different than the others.

that within one moment
you had the power to transform,
to fully damage me.

―――――

———

i fell so deeply for you because you were so
welcoming for me to be myself.

———

———

and when the sun rises, the darkness runs away
to hide. it knows it is not allowed to be seen in the
clear light of day. so in the shadows and corners.
it hides. lingers, stays.

———

———

moving on means letting go.
which becomes easier
each breath i take not next to you.

———

this has brought to me cleansing.
truth.
clarity.

---

i am a lover.
selfishly, selflessly.
i've only had both with you.

———

i am in fact completely committed to you. my soul
belongs to yours. the universe has been preparing
me for you.

i see it has been this way all along.
i am, infatuated by you. in lust, completely in love
with you. it was not always apparent, never really
clear that this was the case. but it is true. i am
meant for you.

i see now that the tears of sorrow, heartache, and
pain i felt all along the way were really my being
longing to be nearer to you. that the mistakes i've
made, the lessons learned, conflicts conquered. they
were all just prepping me to be the best for you.

as i walk through the streets and see the trees, the
flowers, the leaves, i see the perfection of time. the
balance of nature. the growth of love.
in this, i see you.

as i feel the wind brush my face,
the moisture in the air,
the sun on my shoulders,
i feel you.

———

———

at this moment,
there is no place that i'd rather be.
no person who i'd rather be with,
than you.

———

sounds of the birds chirping, stray dogs barking and
fallen leaves crunching under my feet are sweet to
my ears. i hear the poems of your being whisper to
me.

an old soul, peering down as you reach high into the
sky - you are my gift from the heavens above,
a god send to the earth below.
solid and steady,
grounded and stable,
you provide me all that i need.
rooted to the earth, you are one with the universe.
connected, wise, and your age shows throughout.

reveiling with grace your connections.
your maturity, compassion and understanding.
showing your paternal like presence,
your maternal like essence -
producing a love more powerful than the sunshine
that fuels your every cell.

to love
with an opening of heart,
a reveal of soul.
exposing my inner self.
to let down the shield
that keeps others out.
this is a love that i want to give.

i realize that as i see you, you see me
and our longing is diminished.

all the years of rooting and reaching,
swaying in the wind and falling apart
time and time again,
season after season.
this has come to an end.

i heard your cry.
i felt your yearning.
i have seen your soul.

so now - as it has been destined for so long -
we can be reunited in this time,
as we have been searching for all along.

as we close our eyes, and meet palm to palm, the
separation from of our words initiated by silence,
opens up my ears to the sounds of nature that has
tied our souls.

where we have forever and will forever be bound
through all of time, again and again, now united as
one.

do you long for it.
to feel what you once felt.
when you stopped and looked into me.
really stopped. really looked.
intentionally. and saw the depths of me that you've
never seen before.

that one time. the first time.
i saw the beauty you've been smothering.
hiding beneath your busyness.
suffocating with semantics,
false pleasantries.
half crooked smiles and conversations fueled by
weed, whiskey, and wine.

do you long for it.
that one moment.
we stopped time.
when you revealed your deepest
self to me.
when i uncovered the parts of me
that are rarely shown.

anxiety makes the chaos run wild.
because you feel there's no room to relax.

this is untrue.
the only thing needed
is continual connection to your deeper self.

more self love.
less self sacrifice,
more self care.

you house the most beautiful soul,
an ultimate being.
and without connection to yourself
you have no connection to the world.

every breath you inhale
every breath you exhale
is a gift.
don't forget to breathe.
deeply.
from the tips of your toes
to the top of your head.
fingertip to fingertip.
filling all your spaces with this gift.
with gratitude.
with thanks for every moment you have in this life.

this is love.

———

you drink, drown to disconnect.
to numb.
i inhale, smoke to reconnect.
to dig deeper, deeply.
the deepest i can take in.
to see what i've been escaping from
all of my days.
in all of these ways.
i've spent filling my time.
and filing away.
hiding.
haunted.
by the misconnection,
to disconnection.
that you still so comfortably accept.

———

it just feels strangely right.
when i'm with you,
you do all the right things.

you look me in the eye.
waiting, watching.
words flow with ease,
so sweet to receive.

when i am away, still.
you hold me in a space.
where my angst, slows.
my heart. flutters.
softly putters.
my feet, firmly planted.
grounded.

this place, this me.
it feels strangely right.
outside of myself.
comfortable, free.

―――

maybe there's a time
when you admit to yourself
that you were wrong.
that you were wronged.
that you can't fix it all.
that all things come to an end.
maybe that's where the hurting dissolves.
maybe that's where the healing begins.

―――

cut me
till it's deep
enough
that all flows freely.
until it all pours out
and i run dry.

no matter how you push i'm still tied to you. the
love we grew is luring at the bottom of my heart.
trapped, silenced, abandoned by the isolation you
put at the forefront of our existence. you ran,
leaving me and my heart to drown in the sorrows
you sprinkled behind to silence your emotions.
numbed your discontent with vices of self
destruction. and still. somehow. this love that hides
deep in my heart continues to long for you.

———

habitually, you empty your numbness deep into mine.

———

———

you brought me to you to help you heal. to unveil
your inner demons and breathe new life into you.
you asked me to undo this life you've been
smothering with your sorrow.

but listen to me,
i cannot save you.
you,
you must save yourself.

and i will wait for you to do all that needs to be done
in order to see the depths of your own darkness.

i'll stand close by as you wallow in your sadness
and smash your ego into tiny pieces.

my love,
i will wait as you dive deep into your hidden pains.

face to face with them,
until you break.
cave.

i cannot rescue you,
but i will wait close enough that when you look up
you'll come to know,
you were never alone,
all along, i was right there by your side.

opening up the heart,
vulnerability revealed.
opening up,
to visions of desires unfulfilled.
i let you step into my world,
look into my eyes with longing,
seeking to know what i hold inside.

reserved and hesitant i guard from you.
giving only what i think you could expect
keeping my real self, concealed.

but you pushed me, dig deeper.
with your piercing green eyes.
your stare beaconed me, come closer,
with gentleness, caress and care.

and when i let down the walls,
boldly, abruptly, you set me in my place.
trampling my exposed heart with indifference.
you became removed, disengaged.

it all aches.
face caked with humility.
ego, running wild.
mind racing, pacing, stealing hours each night.

yet, casually, you stroll around,
carelessly spewing charm.
a reminder,
warning that deceit always ends the same.

———

be.
gently.
we're all just here.
looking for love.
looking to love.
from where we see it.
to how we see fit.

———

they want me to pretend.
that i'm happy.
that i'm whole.
but not you.
you see me.
and yet,
you still hold me.
as i am.
and this
is why i need you most.

something has touched me so deeply that my soul
aches. it aches so heavy that my big heart breaks.
i feel so deeply that my breath is thick. my throat
clogged with tears that are not slick.

tears that have now been released to slide down my
face. to soak my hair. cleanse my beliefs.

to shake my bones and chill my spine.
tears that are meant to free my being.

a touch so deep that my vision is clouded.
trapped by toxic thoughts poisoning my mind.

days blurred.
lines blurred.
nothing transparent.
nothing solid.

liquified existence.
dripping into a puddle that forms a pool.
to cleanse my being.
to drown my sorrows.
to free my soul.

one hundred twelve

———

when the time is right, you will know and you will
see. when that time comes, all will fall into place.
all will make sense, all will be perfect, just as it is.
you will fall, fall so much. as i have. in love with me.
in love, with your own self too. all in time. so, take
your time. time to grow in you, and into yourself. in
love with you. and when you find love within you,
you will find me.

———

i have met no other
that stirs my soul like you do.
that takes my breath.
tempts me to stop breathing.
as an act to feel nearer
when i am away.
like you do.

———

tell me
how do you heal a heart
that never stops hurting.
how do you free a heart
that never stops feeling.

———

if you held me over the edge
and demanded to know
what am i fighting for.
i'd say truth,
i'd say passion.
i'd scream love.

i'd look you all the way to the center
and i would whisper.
softly.
sweetly.
i am here.
fighting for you.

———

i will not be just another woman.
or one of many.
i will be
the one.
the only.
worshipped greater than any other.

if i let you touch my body.
you have access to my heart.

if you are allowed to penetrate me deeply.
my soul, you too will touch.

caution.
this is a gift.
not given without regard.

———

time could not have been wasted,
i pray that you find the nerve.

———

there are days,
moments,
where you fade
and i cope.
i can see clearly what to do.

but then there are spans of time
where i am reminded of how whole i felt with you.

there's part of me
that hopes you are sitting in your space,
feeling the same way too.

but a bigger part of me hopes you feel complete
without me
that this distance is fulfilling for you.

―――――――

i want to keep you here on my pedestal to have
you close for all of my days.

———

clearly,
i see now
it wasn't you that i fell for.
it was the me that i found,
in the time that i spent near you.

———

self portrait • encinitas, ca • 2019

Kirston,
thank you for your support.
I hope you find PAGES & pieces
here you connect with INSPIRATION
to uncover your own LAYERS ∞
love.
xx, euni

Made in the USA
Middletown, DE
30 June 2019